Teach Your Dog

SCOTS

Funny & surprisingly clever books. Love. Love.

DAWN FRENCH, ACTOR & COMEDIAN

Anne Cakebread not only has the best name in the universe, she has also come up with a brilliantly fun book which will help humans and canines learn new languages.

RICHARD HERRING, COMEDIAN

People are crackers, mate. They think you can teach dogs Scots, when we all know they only speak French.

ARTHUR SMITH, WRITER & COMEDIAN

Teach Your Dog

SCOTS

Anne Cakebread

y lolfa

Thank you to:
Helen, Fred and Wilma, my family, friends and neighbours in St Dogmaels for all their support and encouragement, Carolyn at Y Lolfa and Laura Green of the Scots Language Centre for Scots translations and pronunciations.
Monie thanks.

In memory of Frieda, who started us on the *Teach Your Dog* journey.

First impression 2025

Illustrations and design by Anne Cakebread

ISBN: 978-1-912631-57-5

Published and printed in Wales on paper from well-maintained forests by Y Lolfa Cyf., Talybont, Ceredigion SY24 5HE
e-mail ylolfa@ylolfa.com
website www.ylolfa.com
tel 01970 832 304

I grew up only speaking English.
When I moved to west Wales, I adopted Frieda, a rescue whippet, who would only obey Welsh commands.
Slowly, whilst dealing with Frieda, I realised that I was overcoming my nerves about speaking Welsh aloud, and my Welsh was improving as a result – this gave me the idea of creating a series of books to help others learn languages.
You don't even have to go abroad to practise.
If you haven't got a dog, any pet or soft toy will do: just have fun learning and speaking a new language.

– Anne Cakebread

“Hello”

“Hullo”

pron:

“Huh-low”

“Come here”

“Mon ower here”

pron:

“Moan ower here”

‘ow’ as in ‘how’

"Don't!"

"Dinna dae that!"

pron:

"Din-nah day that!"

"Are you snuggling?"

"Ir ye cooried in?"

pron:

"Ir yi coo-reed in?"

'i' as in 'hit'

"Catch!"

"Get the ba!"

pron:

"Git the bawe!"

'awe' as in 'awesome'

“Fetch!”

“Awa an get it!”

pron:

“Ah-wawe in git it!”

‘awe’
as in
‘awesome’

“No begging!”

“Nae cadgin!”

pron:

“Nay cad-jin!”

MIDGIES
WHISKY

"Sit!"

"Sit nice!"

pron:

"Sit nice!"

"No!"

"Naw!"

pron:

"Nawe!"

'awe'
as in
'awesome'

"Stay there!"

"Bide there!"

pron:

"B*<u>ide</u>* there!"

'ide' as in 'r*<u>ide</u>*'

“Time for a wash”

“Time fir a dicht”

pron:

“Time fir a di<u>ch</u>t”

‘ch’ as in ‘lo<u>ch</u>’

"Go to bed"

"Awa tae yer scratcher"

pron:

"Ah-wawe tay yir scratcher"

'awe' as in 'awesome'

“Time for some food”

“Time fir some scran”

pron:

“Time fir some scran”

"Are you full?"

"Ir ye stappit fu?"

pron:

"Ir yi stapt foo?"

'i' as in 'hit'

"Finished"

"Feenisht"

pron:

"Feenisht"

'i' as in 'hit'

"Good morning"

"Guid mornin"

pron:

"Gid more-nin"

"Goodnight"

"Guid nicht"

pron:

"Gid nicht"

'ch' as in 'loch'

"Leave your ears alone!"

"Lea yer lugs alane!"

pron:

"Lee yir lugs a-lane!"

'a' as in 'ago'

"Let's go..."

"Mon we'll gang oot..."

pron:

"Moan will gang oot..."

“Go down”

“Doon ye go”

pron:

“Doon y_i_ go”

‘i’ as in ‘h_i_t’

"Up you go"

"Up the stair wi ye"

pron:

"Up the stair way yi"

'i' as in 'hit'

“Go straight ahead”

“Gang furrit”

pron:

“Gang fur-it”

"Turn right"

"Birl tae yer richt"

pron:

"Bi_r_l tay yir ri_ch_t"

roll the 'r' a little

'ch' as in 'lo_ch_'

“Turn left”

“Birl tae yer left”

pron:

“Birl tay yir left”

roll the ‘r’ a little

"Are you feeling under the weather today?"

"Ir ye peelie-wally the day?"

pron:

"Ir yi peely-wally the day?"

'i' as in 'hit'

'a' as in 'man'

“I’m just exhausted”

“Jist a bit wabbit”

pron:

“Jist a bit wabbit”

“Get down!”

“Haw you! Get doon!”

pron:

“Haw you! Git doon!”

"Do you want to play?"

"Ir ye wantin tae pley?"

pron:

"Ir yi wahn-tin tay pliy?"

'i' as in 'hit'

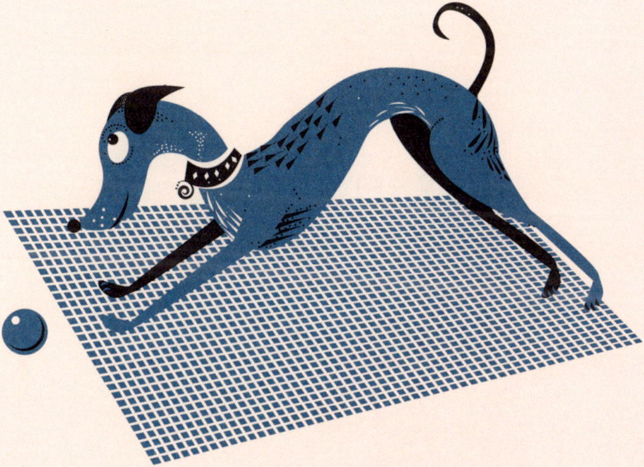

"Lie down!"

"Lie doon!"

pron:

"Lie doon!"

"Give me a paw!"

"Gies a paw!"

pron:

"Geez a paw!"

'G' as in 'get'

"Can I have the ball?"

"Can Ah hae the ba?"

pron:

"Kin Ah hay the bawe?"

'awe' as in 'awesome'

"Can I have a
potato scone?"

**"Can Ah hae a
tattie scone?"**

pron:

***"Kin Ah hay a
tattie skon?"***

*'o'
as in
'hot'*

“Very clever”

“Fair crafty”

pron:

“Fair crafty”

$x+1$
B
4
$x+11$
A
C
$2x+6$
$A=B+C$
$B=4(x+1)$
$=4x+4$
$C=(x+11-4)(2x+6)$
$(x+7)(2x+6)$
$(2x^2+14x+6x+42)$
$(2x^2+20x+42)$
$B+C=$
$2x^2+20x+42+4x+4$
$2x^2+24x+46$
$A=2x^2+24x+46$

"It's warm, isn't it?"

"Gey warm, int it?"

pron:

"Giy wahrm, int it?"

"It's cold"

"It's baltic"

pron:

"It's baltic"

“It’s hot!”

“Taps aff!”

pron:

“Taps ahff!”

"It's pouring"

"It's teemin doon"

pron:

"It's tee-min doon"

"Do you want a stroke?"

"Ir ye wantin a clap?"

pron:

"Ir yi wantin a clap?"

'i' as in 'hit'

'a' as in 'man'

“Who’s snoring?”

“Whase neb’s rattlin?”

pron:

“Whahs nebz rattlin?”

make a slight blowing sound with your lips

zz
zzz
zz

"Are you comfortable?"

"Comfy, aye?"

pron:

"Come-fay, eye?"

60103

"I won't be long"

"Ah willna be lang"

pron:

"Ah will-nah be lang"

"Be quiet!"

"Wheesht!"

pron:

"__Wh__-ee-shhh-t!"

make a slight blowin sound with your lips

"Who did that?"

"Och – wha did thon?"

pron:

"Och — whawe did thown?"

'ch' as in 'loch'

'awe' as in 'awesome'

'ow' as in 'show'

make a slight blowing sound with your lips

'th' as in 'this'

"You'll have to wait for the loo"

"Ye'll can wait fir the cludgie"

pron:

"Yill kin wait fir the cluhdji"

'i' as in 'hit'

'i' as in 'hit'

1

“yin”

pron:

“yin”

2

“twa”

pron:

“tw<u>awe</u>”

‘awe’
as in
‘<u>awe</u>some’

3

“three”

pron:

“three”

4

“fower”

pron:

“fowir”

‘ow’
as in
‘how’

5

"five"

pron:

"five"

6

"sax"

pron:

"sahx"

7

“seevin”

pron:

“seevin”

8

“echt”

pron:

“ehcht”

‘ch’ as in ‘loch’

9

"nine"

pron:

"nine"

10

“ten”

pron:

“ten”

"Thank you"

"Monie thanks"

pron:

"Moan-eh thanks"

"Merry Christmas"

"A blythe yule tae ye"

pron:

"A bly-th yool tay yi"

'th' as in 'thin'

'i' as in 'hit'

"Live long and prosper!"

"Lang may yer lum reek!"*

pron:

"Lang may yir lum reek!"

'um' as in 'sum'

*used to wish people luck on special occasions, especially Hogmanay

"Happy Birthday, old one"

"Happy Birthday, auld yin"

pron:

"Happy Birthday, auld yin"

"I love you"

"Ah shuirly luve ye"

pron:

"Ah share-lay luv yi"

'i' as in 'hit'

"Goodbye"

"Cheerio"

pron:

"Cheery-oh"

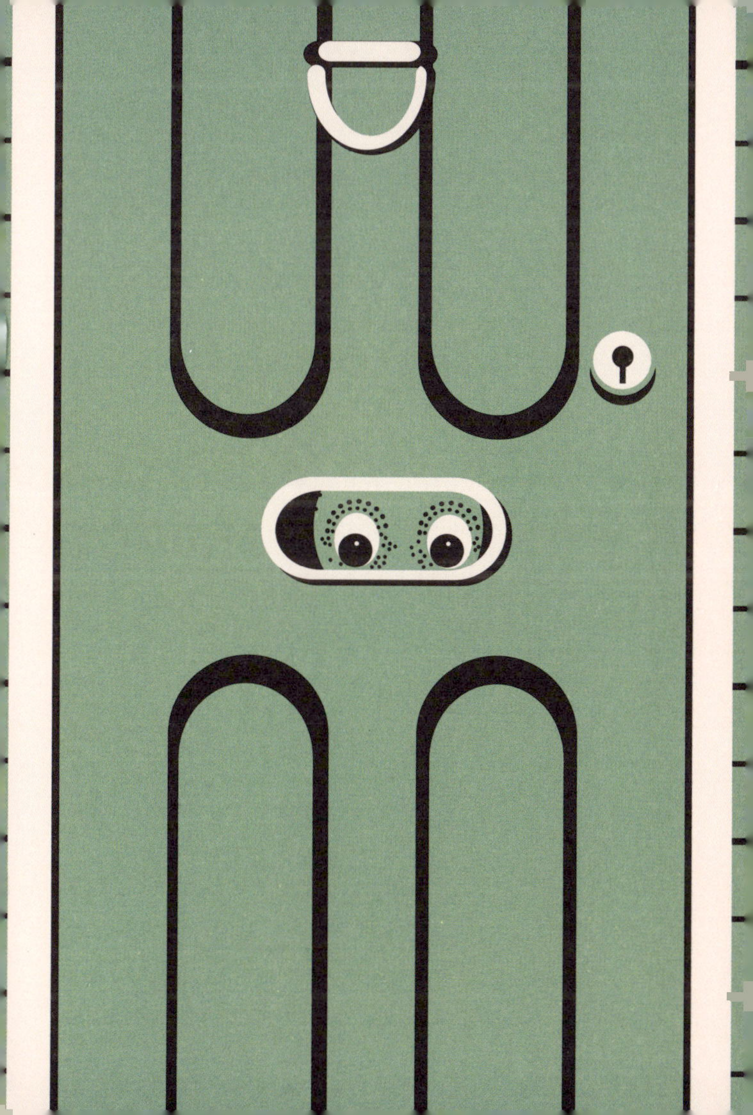

Titles in this series include:

Teach Your Dog British Sign Language
Teach Your Cat Cornish
Teach Your Dog Cornish
Teach Your Dog French
Teach Your Cat Gaelic
Teach Your Dog Gaelic
Teach Your Dog German
Teach Your Dog Gog: North Wales Welsh
Teach Your Cat Guernesiais
Teach Your Cat Irish
Teach Your Dog Irish
Teach Your Dog Italian
Teach Your Dog Japanese
(Rugby Travel Edition)
Teach Your Dog Jèrriais
Teach Your Dog Korean
Teach Your Cat Manx
Teach Your Dog Māori
Teach Your Dog Spanish
Teach Your Cat Welsh
Teach Your Dog Welsh

More coming soon!